# DISCARDED

# COOL

# Paper

# PROJECTS

Creative Ways to Upcycle Your Trash into Treasure

A Division of ABDO
**ABDO**
Publishing Company

PAM SCHEUNEMANN

visit us at www.abdopublishing.com

Published by ABDO Publishing Company, a division of ABDO, P.O. Box 398166, Minneapolis, Minnesota 55439. Copyright © 2013 by Abdo Consulting Group, Inc. International copyrights reserved in all countries. No part of this book may be reproduced in any form without written permission from the publisher. Checkerboard Library™ is a trademark and logo of ABDO Publishing Company.

Printed in the United States of America, North Mankato, Minnesota
062012
092012

 PRINTED ON RECYCLED PAPER

DESIGN AND PRODUCTION: ANDERS HANSON, MIGHTY MEDIA, INC.
SERIES EDITOR: LIZ SALZMANN
PHOTO CREDITS: SHUTTERSTOCK

The following manufacturers/names appearing in this book are trademarks: Americana® Multi-Purpose™ Sealer, Artist's Loft™, Avery®, Elmer's®, Mod Podge®, Sharpie®

LIBRARY OF CONGRESS CATALOGING-IN-PUBLICATION DATA

Scheunemann, Pam, 1955-
  Cool paper projects : creative ways to upcycle your trash into treasure / Pam Scheunemann.
      pages cm -- (Cool trash to treasure)
  Includes index.
  ISBN 978-1-61783-436-3
  1.  Paper work--Juvenile literature. 2.  Salvage (Waste, etc.)-- Juvenile literature.  I. Title.
  TT870.S294 2012
  745.593--dc23
                              2012000678

# TABLE of CONTENTS

# TRASH

## ⓉⓄ *Treasure*

### THE SKY'S THE LIMIT

The days of throwing everything in the trash are long over. Recycling has become a part of everyday life. To recycle means to use something again or to find a new use for it. By creating treasures out of trash, we are also *upcycling*. This is a term used to **describe** making useful items out of things that may have been thrown away.

## Permission and Safety

- Always get **permission** before making any type of craft at home.

- Ask if you can use the tools and materials needed.

- Ask for help when you need it.

- Be careful when using knives, scissors, or other sharp objects.

## Be Prepared

- Read the entire activity before you begin.

- Make sure you have everything you need to do the project.

- Keep your work area clean and organized.

- Follow the directions carefully.

- Clean up after you are finished for the day.

Most paper can be recycled. But instead of recycling your unwanted paper, why not give it new life? There are many ways you can upcycle paper. See what you can come up with. The sky's the limit.

In this book you'll find great ideas to upcycle different kinds of paper. Make them just like they appear here or use your own ideas. You can make them for yourself or as gifts for others. These projects use easy-to-find tools and materials.

# A FRESH LOOK AT

# PAPER

T here are many sources of paper. Magazines, newspaper, junk mail, envelopes, greeting cards, candy wrappers, and wrapping paper are just a few. All of these types of paper can be upcycled. Here are some things you can make with unwanted paper.

## Cards & Calendars

- PAPER EMBELLISHMENTS
- ENVELOPES
- NEW CARDS

# Newspaper

- GIFT BAGS
- WRAPPING PAPER
- SEEDLING POTS

# Magazines

- ENVELOPES
- BOWS
- **COLLAGES**

# Maps

- PICTURE MATS
- ORIGAMI
- PAPER WEAVING

# Tissue Paper

- DECOUPAGE
- PAPER FLOWERS
- BOWLS

# TOOLS & MATERIALS

**1-INCH (3 CM) HOLE PUNCH**

**ACRYLIC PAINT**

**ALL-PURPOSE SEALER**

**ARTIST'S CANVAS**

**CARDBOARD**

**CURTAIN ROD**

**FOAM PAINTBRUSHES**

**GLUE STICK**

**JAR LIDS**

**JARS**

**LABELS**

**LARGE PAPER CLIPS**

**LUCITE ROLLER**

**MAGAZINES**

**MASKING TAPE**

**MOD PODGE**

# If you don't know what something is, turn back to these pages!

**NEWSPAPER**

**OLD FRAME**

**OLD MAP**

**PAINT CHIPS**

**PAINT PENS**

**PLASTIC WRAP**

**RIBBON**

**ROUND CHOPSTICK**

**RULER**

**SANDING BLOCK**

**SMALL PAINTBRUSH**

**SPLIT RINGS**

**STICKERS**

**USED ENVELOPES**

**WHITE ADDRESS LABELS**

**WOODEN SKEWERS**

## STUFF YOU'LL NEED

- **JAR WITH LID**
- **DECORATIVE PAPER SCRAPS**
- **MARKER**
- **RULER**
- **SCISSORS**
- **CARDBOARD**
- **Mod Podge**
- **FOAM BRUSH**

# paper toppers

## Make cool lids in just a few minutes!

1   Wash the lid and jar. Remove any labels and let them dry. Find paper scraps that you like. They can be bits of wrapping paper, **origami** paper, or scrapbook paper.

2   Put the lid upside down on the back of a piece of decorative paper. Trace a circle around it.

3   Measure the height of the sides of the lid. Double the measurement. Make several marks around the circle that distance away from it. Use the marks to draw a larger circle around the first circle. Cut out the larger circle.

4   Make cuts from the edge of the paper to the inner circle. Make them about 1/4 inch (.6 cm) apart.

5   Spread Mod Podge over the inner circle. Press the jar lid on top of it. Turn it over and smooth out any wrinkles in the paper.

6   Place the lid on a piece of cardboard. Brush Mod Podge on a couple of the strips of paper. Fold the strips one at a time over the edge of the lid. Continue gluing and folding the remaining strips.

7   Turn the lid over. Cover the top and sides with Mod Podge. Let it dry completely before putting the lid back on the jar.

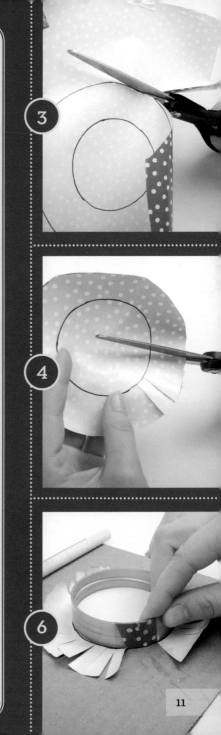

11

- DECORATIVE
  AND PLAIN
  PAPER SCRAPS

- RULER

- PENCIL

- SCISSORS

- GLUE STICK

- LUCITE ROLLER
  OR SMOOTH-
  SIDED GLASS

- HOLE PUNCH

- 8 INCHES
  (20 CM) RIBBON

# WOVEN PAPER BOOKMARK

Makes a really cool design!

1.  First you need to make a **template**. Start with a plain, 3 by 5-inch (8 by 13 cm) piece of paper. Fold it in half **lengthwise**.

2.  Draw a straight line 1/2 inch (1.3 cm) from the fold. Draw another line 1 inch (2.6 cm) from the fold.

3.  Make marks along the folded edge every 1/4 inch (.6 cm). Make the same marks along the 1-inch line.

4.  Position the paper with the fold toward you. Start on the right side. Line the ruler up between the second mark on the 1-inch line and the corner of the fold.

5.  Draw a line from the 1-inch line to the corner. Move the ruler so it is lined up between the third mark on the 1-inch line and the first mark on the fold. Draw a line from the 1/2-inch line to the fold. Move the ruler so it is lined up between the fourth mark on the 1-inch line and the second mark on the fold. Draw a line from the 1-inch line to the fold. Keep moving the ruler and drawing lines, alternating between long and short lines. Stop when you get to the left side of the paper.

*Continued on the next page*

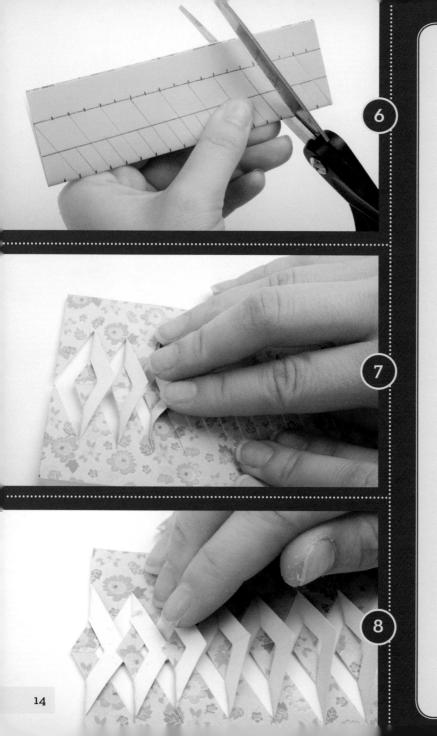

**6** Cut a piece of decorative paper to 3 by 5 inches (8 by 13 cm). Fold it in half **lengthwise**. Wrap the fold of the **template** over the fold of the decorative paper. Cut on the **diagonal** lines.

**7** Remove the template and unfold the decorative paper. Lay it down with the fold facing up. The diagonal cuts will form points. Carefully fold the wider points down. Crease the edges. Cut off any extra paper at the ends.

**8** Use the glue stick to put a little glue on the tips of the points you folded down. Tuck them under the points facing the other way. Press each one firmly.

9   Cut a piece of colored paper a little larger than 3 by 5 inches (8 by 13 cm).

10  Use the glue stick to cover the back of the woven decorative paper with glue. Press it in the center of the colored paper. Roll over it with a Lucite roller or smooth-sided glass.

11  Punch a hole at the top of the weaving.

12  Fold the ribbon in half. Push the fold through the hole from front to back. Wrap the ends over the top and through the fold.

- **5 ENVELOPES
  THAT ARE THE
  SAME SIZE**

- **GLUE STICK**

- **SCISSORS**

- **RIBBON**

- **LABELS**

- **MARKER**

- **STICKERS**

- **COLORED
  PAPER**

# ENVELOPE ORGANIZER

Wrap up your paper bits in this!

1. Spread glue on the inside of one envelope flap. Lay the second envelope on top of it. Press firmly. Spread glue on the flap of that envelope. Lay the third envelope on top of it. Press firmly. Add the fourth envelope the same way.

2. Make small cuts in the top and bottom of the fifth envelope. The cuts should be as wide as the ribbon. Push the ribbon through both cuts.

3. Spread glue on the outside of the fourth envelope's flap. Press it onto the pocket of the fifth envelope. Let the glue dry.

4. Write the content of each envelope on the labels. Stick a label on the pocket of each envelope. Decorate the envelopes with stickers and bits of colored paper.

5. Fold the envelopes **accordion**-style and tie the ribbon around them. Or use the ribbon to hang them up as a wall organizer.

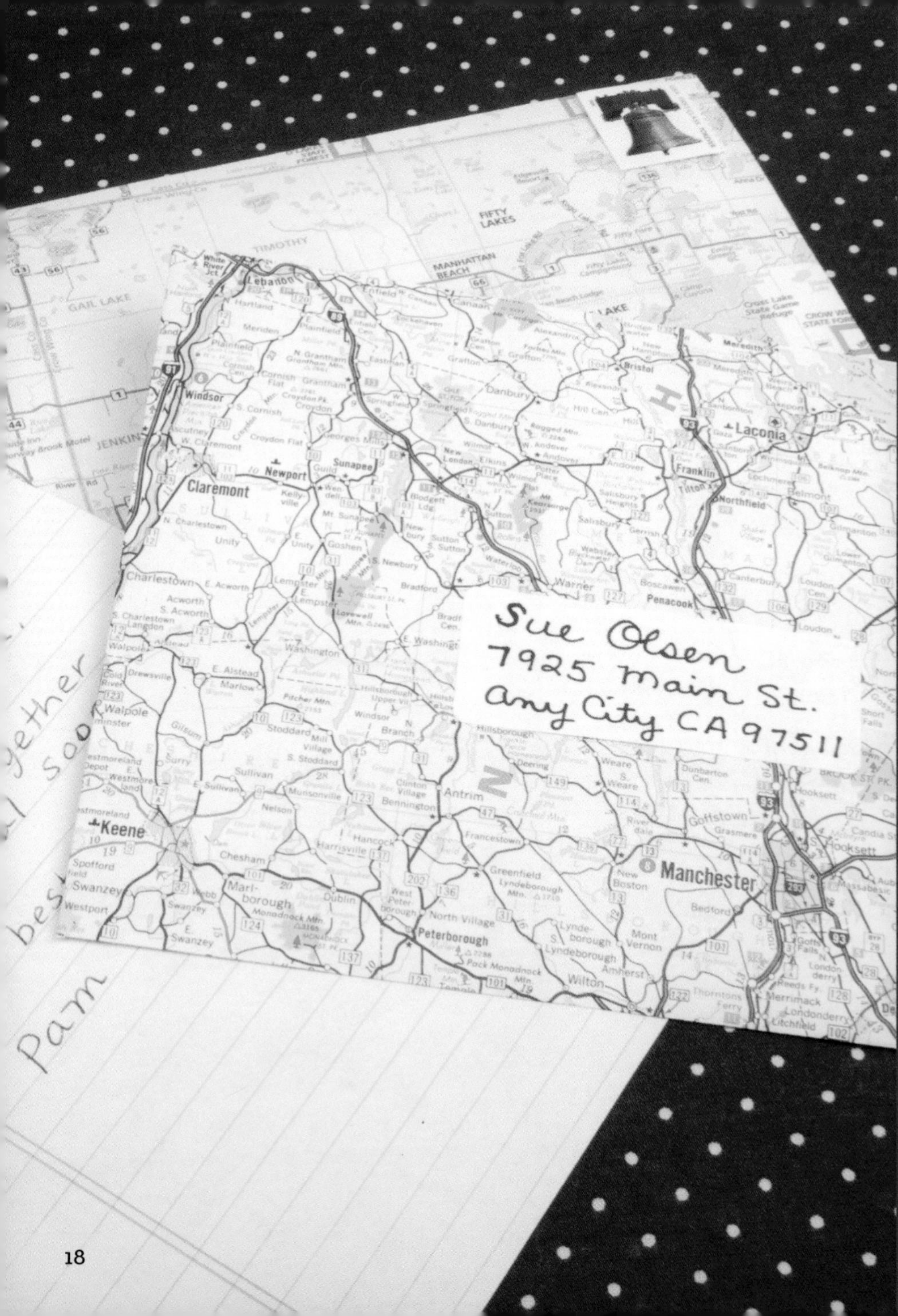

- **ENVELOPE**

- **MAP**

- **MARKER**

- **SCISSORS**

- **RULER**

- **DINNER KNIFE**

- **GLUE STICK**

- **WHITE ADDRESS
  LABELS**

Sue Olsen
7925 Main St.
Any City CA 97511

# MaP-VELOPE

## Help your cards find their way!

1. Carefully open up the envelope along the seams. Unfold it completely.

2. Lay the envelope on the map. Trace around the envelope. Cut it out just inside the lines, so they won't show. Lay the map cutout face down on the table.

3. Look at where the folds are in the envelope you traced. You'll need to fold your map envelope the same way. Place the ruler where you want to make a fold. Run the back of a dinner knife along the ruler. This **scores** the paper where you will fold it. Continue to score the map everywhere it needs to be folded.

4. Fold in the side flaps. Put glue along both edges of the bottom flap. Fold the bottom flap up and press it to the side flaps. Let the glue dry.

5. When you are ready to mail something, put it in the envelope and glue the top flap down. Use labels to add the mailing address and your return address.

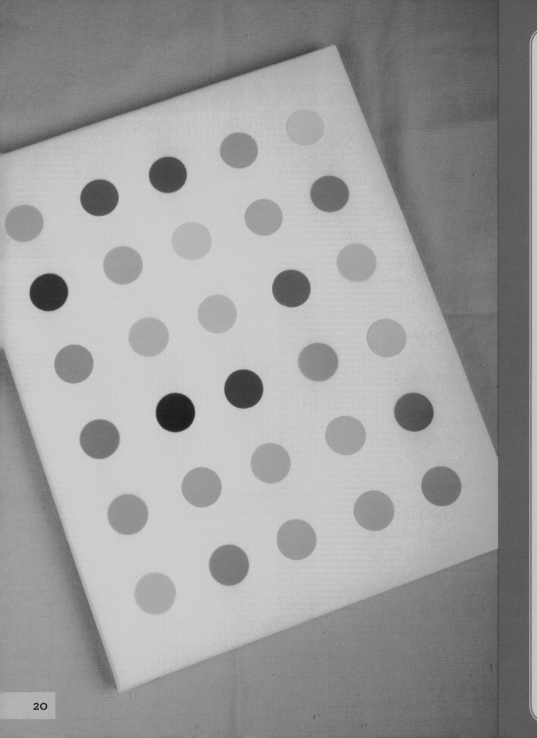

## STUFF YOU'LL NEED

- NEWSPAPER
- ARTIST'S CANVAS
- ACRYLIC PAINT
- FOAM BRUSH
- COLORED PAINT CHIPS
- 1-INCH CIRCLE PUNCH
- GLUE STICK

# PAINT CHIP POP ART

Pop goes the easel!

1. Spread newspaper over your work surface. Paint the whole artist's **canvas**. Paint a couple of coats. Let the paint dry after each coat.

2. Use the circle punch to cut circles out of paint chips.

3. Arrange the paint chip circles on the canvas. Glue them down. Let the glue dry.

4. Find a great place to hang your art!

## STUFF YOU'LL NEED

- **MAGAZINES**
- **SCISSORS**
- **RULER**
- **LARGE PAPER CLIPS**
- **GLUE STICK**
- **SPLIT RINGS**
- **CURTAIN ROD**

### How Many Rings & Paper Clips?

Measure the width of the space where you will hang the curtain. You will need one split ring per 1 inch (2.5 cm). That is how many chains you will make.

Measure the height of the space. For each chain, you will need one paper clip per 2 inches (5 cm) in height.

# SCRAP PAPER CURTAIN

## Hang it in a doorway or window!

1   Find some colorful magazine pages. Cut out rectangles that are 1¹/2 by 2 inches (4 by 5 cm). You will need a rectangle for each paper clip.

2   Push a short side of one of the rectangles under the middle of a paper clip.

3   Wrap the paper all the way around the paper clip. Make sure the side you want to show is facing out. Run the glue stick along the end of the rectangle. Press it down firmly.

4   Attach another paper clip to the first paper clip. Wrap it with a paper rectangle the same way you did the first one. Keep adding paper clips and wrapping them with paper. Stop when the chain is as long as the height of the space.

5   Repeat steps 2 through 4 to make a chain for each split ring. Attach a split ring to one end of each chain. Put the split rings on the curtain rod. You may need to have an adult help you hang the curtain rod.

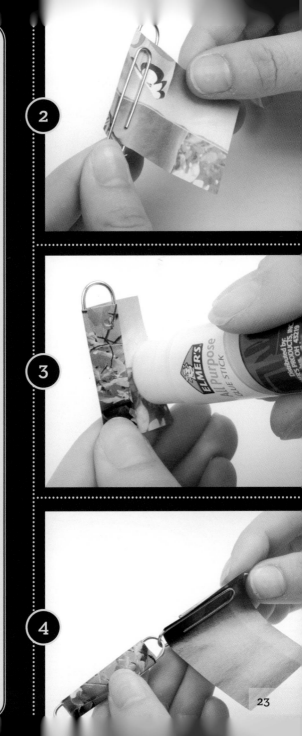

## STUFF YOU'LL NEED

- **MAGAZINES**
- **ROUND CHOPSTICK**
- **GLUE STICK**
- **WOODEN SKEWER**
- **SCISSORS**
- **OLD FRAME**
- **FOAM BRUSH**
- **MOD PODGE**

# Magazine Roll Frame

## Upcycle an old frame!

1. Find some colorful magazine pages. Look for pages with outer edges that have colors you like. Rip out the pages.

2. Lay a page down with the colored edge you like face down. Set the chopstick on the torn edge of the page. Use the glue stick to put a line of glue about 1/2 inch (1 cm) in front of the chopstick.

3. Roll the page tightly around the chopstick. Put glue along the end of the paper. Press it to the roll. Use the wooden skewer to push the chopstick out of the roll of paper.

4. Repeat steps 2 and 3 to make more colorful rolls of paper.

5. Remove the backing and glass from the frame. Cut the paper rolls into pieces and arrange them on the frame. Cover the frame completely with rolls of paper. Glue the rolls onto the frame. Let the glue dry.

6. Cover the frame with a couple of coats of Mod Podge. Let it dry after each coat. Then add your favorite photo!

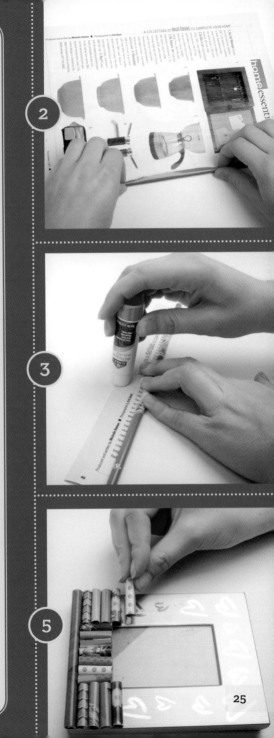

## STUFF YOU'LL NEED

- NEWSPAPER
- BOWL
- PLASTIC WRAP
- MASKING TAPE
- JAR
- FOAM BRUSH
- MOD PODGE
- WHITE RECYCLED PAPER
- SANDING BLOCK
- PAPER TOWEL
- SCISSORS
- ACRYLIC PAINT
- SMALL PAINTBRUSH
- MARKER OR PAINT PEN
- ALL-PURPOSE SEALER

# painted paper bowl

## Turn newspaper into a bowl!

1. Spread newspaper over your work surface. Cover the outside of the bowl with plastic wrap.

2. Pull the plastic wrap so it is as smooth as possible. Tape the edges to the inside of the bowl.

3. Tear newspaper into strips. Place the bowl upside down on top of the jar. Make sure the jar is tall enough that the bowl doesn't touch the table.

4. Brush a coat of Mod Podge on the plastic wrap. Brush a little Mod Podge on a newspaper strip. Stick the strip to the bowl. Brush a coat of Mod Podge over the strip. Keep adding Mod Podge and strips of newspaper until the bowl is covered. Let it dry for an hour. Add two more layers of Mod Podge and newspaper strips. Let it dry for an hour between each layer.

*Continued on the next page*

5 Put on a final layer of paper and Mod Podge. This time use white paper instead of newspaper. There can be writing on one side of the white paper. Just stick the printed side to the bowl. Let the bowl dry for at least nine hours.

6 Use a sanding block to smooth out any rough spots. Don't rub too hard or you'll wear the surface down. Wipe the bowl with a damp paper **towel** to get rid of the dust.

7 Remove the plastic wrap from the bowl.

8 Gently remove the paper bowl from the plastic wrap.

9  Trim around the edge of the bowl to even it out. Or just leave it as is for a more natural look.

10  Paint the bowl white. Let it dry.

11  Coat the inside of the bowl with colored paint. Add some cool shapes. Let it dry. Outline the shapes with a black paint pen or marker.

12  Put the bowl upside down on the jar. Paint the outside of the bowl. Let the paint dry completely. You can use the same color as the inside or a different color. Paint some more shapes. Let it dry. Use paint pens or markers to add other decorations.

13  Cover the bowl with a coat of all-purpose sealer. Let it dry completely.

This bowl is not safe to serve food in, unless the food is wrapped so it doesn't touch the bowl.

# CONCLUSION

Now you know what upcycling is all about. What hidden gems do you have around your house? Do you have relatives who need their **attic** cleaned? What about **garage** and yard sales? Are there **thrift stores** and reuse centers near you? These are all great sources for materials that you can upcycle!

There are many benefits to upcycling. You can make some really great stuff for yourself or gifts for your family and friends. You can save useful things from going into the trash. And the best part is, you don't have to spend a lot of money doing it!

So keep your eyes and ears open for new ideas. There are many Web sites that are all about recycling and upcycling. You might find ideas on TV or in magazines. There are endless ways that you can make something beautiful and useful from **discarded** materials. Remember, the sky's the limit!

# GLOSSARY

**ACCORDION** – folded back and forth like the sides of an accordion.

**ATTIC** – a room right under the roof of a building.

**CANVAS** – a piece of cloth that is stretched over a frame and used as a surface for a painting.

**DESCRIBE** – to tell about something with words or pictures.

**DIAGONAL** – from one corner of a square or rectangle to the opposite corner.

**DISCARD** – to throw away.

**GARAGE** – a room or building that cars are kept in. A *garage sale* is a sale that takes place in a garage.

**LENGTHWISE** – in the direction of the longest side.

**ORIGAMI** – the Japanese art of paper folding.

**PERMISSION** – when a person in charge says it's okay to do something.

**SCORE** – to mark with a line or scratch.

**TEMPLATE** – a shape you draw or cut around to copy it onto something else.

**THRIFT STORE** – a store that sells used items, especially one that is run by a charity.

**TOWEL** – a cloth or paper used for cleaning or drying.

# Web sites

To learn more about cool craft projects, visit ABDO Publishing Company on the World Wide Web at www.abdopublishing.com. Web sites about creative ways for upcycling trash are featured on our Book Links page. These links are routinely monitored and updated to provide the most current information available.

# INDEX